A Pom Cyclist in Australasia
Part one
New Zealand

www.pennyworldcycles.co.uk

PennyWorldCycleTours

Copyright © 2016 Paul Davenport

www.pennyworldcycles.co.uk

A Pom Cyclist in Australasia

New Zealand

After 30 years I was heading back to Auckland to relive one of the most enjoyable cycle rides of my life. Would it be as good after all this time? Would I even recognise all the places I had found so stunningly beautiful as I wandered around the coastlines of both main islands? Was the figure eight route taken then still possible now? Was the *back wind all the way* theory of the 1980s real, or just an illusion? On the long tiring journey on the plane I'd had plenty of time to cast my mind back to Papa New Guinea in the 80s, when the planning for my first trip had taken place…

A sickening thump caused the twenty stone sow to collapse in a heap. The young bridegroom had hit it on top of the head, right between the eyes, with a huge club. Two older men came forward with sharp looking knifes. One of them lifted the sows eyelids to ensure it was out cold before both of them hacked it into lumps of pork, wrapped them in banana leaves, before carefully placing the meat onto the hot stones at the bottom of a previously prepared pit. The pit was then covered with more banana leaves, soil, and the whole thing left to cook while the wedding celebrations continued.

It was only a few days before when Clive, my brother, had been joking about me ending up in a stewing pot like the missionaries in old newspaper cartoons, as he drove me down from Yorkshire to Heathrow to see me off to New Guinea. His loud voice had turned heads as he bellowed over the crowded departure hall, "If you have a choice between the pot and the spit, take the pot every time. If it has to be the spit, take the club anaesthetic." In this bloody introduction to PNG (Papua New Guinea), the club anaesthetic did seem to work.

Key to all life's celebrations in PNG are the pigs. Wealth is measured in pigs. Not how many you have, but how many you give away. The most important pigs of all are those destined to be part of a wedding feast. Anyone who is unfortunate enough to bump a pig with their car will always hit a 'bride pig', this is guaranteed, and it will cost them a great deal of money.

This was my first overseas teaching job, and was at Port Moresby International High School, known to the pupils as Pom High. It was a wonderful school, and like everything of value in PNG, had a security fence all the way around and guards to control the movement in and out of the compound. One of our guards was the man that was getting married, and I, along with several other members of staff, had been invited to the wedding. The path to the village where the wedding took place was so steep that at times we had to use our hands to climb the hill. Remarkably, my memory of the wedding, on the precipitous hillside, was only of rhythmic drums, scanty but colourful costumes, and erotic dancing.

The island of New Guinea is huge, mountainous, and covered in difficult to penetrate jungle. The hundreds of years of isolation of small pockets of humanity has resulted in many distinct languages – astonishingly, it is said to have one third of the world's languages. Anyone able to climb the precipitous mountains, hack their way through the dense vegetation, and find the next village, would be eaten. The people of New Guinea were, almost in living memory, cannibals. Not the sort of place, until recent times, to open a travel agency.

In PNGs modern world, primary school education has become common, secondary less common, and tertiary rare. In the 1980s, a well- educated citizen could find a decent job in the big towns of Lae in the North or Port Moresby in the south. Hundreds of people left the security of their isolated village communities with the hope of finding work and independence. To communicate they used Neo-Melanesian – better known as Pidgin English. Sadly, while many, mostly the better educated, did find work, the others did not. Young men did not want the considerable loss of face brought about by returning home. Usually they received help from anyone from their own village who had found a job. In Pidgin these were their *wantoks* (one talk) – people who spoke the same language. *Wantoks* were very close. They looked like brothers and sisters, and because of the small size of their villages, were closely related, and they felt obliged to help each other.

As unemployment became more common so did crime. Often big gangs of stealing, murdering, raping, young men would create hell. Eventually they would be rounded up by the police and find themselves in jail. It was not uncommon, because they had found a *Wantok* on the prison staff, for them to escape and be rapidly back to their life of crime.

The political classes provided a poor example. Corruption was, and I believe still is, rife. The country is rich in gold, copper and timber – giving ample scope for kickbacks.

In case I've made this sound like hell on earth, and to some people it was, for me it was wonderful. The grand plan had been to cycle around the world and as I didn't have any money, the only way was to work my passage.

I had found an excellent teaching post. Being at the opposite side of the world from the UK made it a clean break and a good starting point. And most important, I was to experience a very different culture. On the downside, there are hardly any roads at all on the whole island of New Guinea. Not the perfect place for a cyclist.

Before the rainy season there were deep rich coloured flowers everywhere. When the rains came, the potholed roads would steam; smells, not noticed before, would bombard the senses; and there was the squelch of huge cane toads being squashed on the road by passing traffic.

The 1930s experiment with cane toads in Australia had also taken place in PNG. It was a total disaster in both countries. Not only did they fail to protect the sugar cane crop as they were supposed to – the toads found far more wonderful things to eat; they themselves were eaten by predators and their slow acting poison gradually wiped out many indigenous animals who were unable to relate their sickness to the cane toads. They have now spread, in their millions, over a huge area of New Guinea and Australia. I've seen many Australian children pick these huge toads up like a doll and lay them on their backs. The toads close their eyes and seem to go to sleep. OK I suppose providing the kids wash their hands before they eat.

In the mind set of local people there is no distinction between cold-blooded murder and killing someone in a road accident. While it might just be possible, with loads of cash, to get away with hitting a pig, the advice was to catch the first plane out of the country if you hit a person.

Locals would have vendettas over accidental deaths for years. In the end these were often settled with a feast and an exchange of pigs.

The most important sport in PNG is rugby league, an Australian import. Team support is tribal, and the place to be seen for any politician wanting re-election. On one occasion, the Minister of Sport no less, dropped his trousers and flashed his bum at the opposition. Several people were killed in the riot that followed. No doubt it was all sorted out in the end with an exchange of pigs. Anyway, if you're a politician, with enough pigs to give away, you can get away with murder.

6.5To keep fit, John (the head of Geography) and I would spend our evenings running. About once a month there would be a triathlon, one of the few times I got a decent workout on the bike. We did get a couple of weeks off when I was able to fly out to Cairns, and wander with my bike and tent around the Atherton Tablelands in Queensland. Other than that, I was heading for New Zealand during the Christmas break with little cycling fitness. John came up with a grand plan. As a Kiwi and a geographer, he had a detailed knowledge of the weather systems. We sat down and planned my route together, with the aim of getting a back wind all the way around the two main islands.

-

A shock was waiting for me when I unpacked my gear at Auckland Airport. It had taken one hell of a battering. My lights, my charging system for my Garmin and iPhone, were damaged beyond local repair, but more importantly, the front forks had been crushed so that getting the front wheel into place was near impossible. Two huge men managed to spring the forks just enough for me to slot in the wheel. It would run out of line for the whole trip, but what the hell, I could now ride the bike.
This was a complete contrast to 30 years ago when bikes didn't have to be packed in boxes to be anything like safe. Flying into Auckland from PNG via Cairns, I had then to let some air out of the tyres and simply hand the bike over, and it landed without a scratch. Now, with the huge aircraft used on these long journeys, when, as happened in Sydney, someone didn't turn up for the flight and everything had to

be taken out of the plane then repacked, ground staff might be less than careful!

A slight distant memory informed me of a campsite on the Great South Road, which after twenty minutes of riding, I managed to find – the road not the campsite. I then made the mistake of using the Garmin. I couldn't for the life of me remember what campsites were called in NZ. In Australia they are almost always called Caravan Parks. My battered hands from getting the front wheel in place, found it almost impossible to type anything into the Garmin. After a lot of effort I managed *camping,* then foolishly followed directions to a camping equipment shop, which was closed. I gave up, and looked for a motel. My first move in the motel was to lose a screw from my glasses, I gave up again, took a shower, went to bed and slept for a long time.

Using a spare, rather old pair of glasses I found in my handlebar bag, my glasses were repaired with cotton and epoxy resin, before heading down the Great South Road. A short distance beyond where I attempted to input something into the Garmin, I found the campsite. It was called Manukau Holiday Park. I was later to find that Holiday Parks, Motor Camps, and even Motels, would often have camping facilities, and this would be the only time I would have trouble finding a campsite except in Auckland. As well as the above campsites, which tend to be privately owned, there are also DOC campsites, which are not. Almost every privately owned campsite has facilities beyond what we usually find in Europe or North America. A kitchen, with the sort of equipment you would have at home: a microwave, toaster, electric and gas oven, kettle (and often also on-tap boiling water), a fridge, freezer etc.

There is often a TV room, a place to relax with frequently a book exchange, which I was to use a lot. The DOC campsites are usually more basic – more like we find in Europe, where your own cooking equipment is required. Unlike Europe, a restaurant belonging to the campsite is rare, so food should be bought on route.

Heading out of Auckland, it didn't take long to spot the first major change – the traffic. My route 30 years ago had taken me south along route 1 to Hamilton. For a major route, this had been almost traffic free. Now it was a motorway, and I found myself on the 22, a road that twisted and turned around, and for my jet-lagged legs, tough climbs. Luckily, before it got too remote, I bought some food in a dairy. The term *dairy* in towns is not used for places where cows are milked, but for what we would call a corner shop, or small supermarket. I also bought myself a breakfast in the same block of shops. This was a very good move as there was going to be nowhere to buy anything for a very long time.

At a pleasant rest area, alongside a river and before a long bridge, I was tempted to stop, put up the tent, and sleep. It seemed to be a stopping point for canoes, and they probably did camp there. However, I felt I should press on and cover some distance on my first ride of the tour.

The wind was some help as the road meandered around and over hills as it headed south. Once in a while there were little villages, but these consisted of a few houses, no shops, and I suspect most people were at work in a bigger towns as they were very few of them around.

In the ditch at the side of the road I saw some movement. For a short distance I walked alongside a hedgehog as it headed in the same direction as me. I would see plenty more dead on the roads, and only one other living example.

Like many other creatures in NZ it must have been brought over by settlers who wanted to create a familiar environment in their new home to the home they had left behind. I was about to get back on the bike again when a cycle tourist cycled up the hill towards me. He said he was going to try and get to Raglan. I looked on the map, it was still one hell of a long way to go, and if I intended to do the same I would have to get some more water. It had been a very hot day and I was in danger of dehydration. Just in front of me was a lady mowing the grass. When I stopped to ask her about water she pointed to another woman also grass mowing a couple of hundred metres down the road. "This was once a school", the second woman told me, "and it was a gift to the education authority from a member of our community, when the school closed they let us buy it back. If you would like I can open up the toilet block and you can camp here." This was a wonderful offer, and I didn't turn it down. I had ridden just 100km, and for day one, that was plenty.

School camp

The next morning, after coffee and porridge, cooked while sheltering from the rain, I was on my way again. With the rain came a strong headwind, but until the junction was reached where it was either left to Hamilton or right to Raglan, I hadn't made up my mind. Without any real thought, I headed right, and drifted further from my 80s route. In the 80s these roads would most likely have been gravel, and in the restricted time I had then, out of the question. My reward came almost at once, a stall to buy some excellent coffee and a dairy to stock up with food. The rain stopped and I was soon in Raglan. I found the campsite over a bridge from the town, on an island, pitched my tent and headed back over the bridge, first to buy fruit and then to get a meal.

Seaside restaurant

The big plan was to cook my own food most of the time, with an occasional bought meal. By and large I stuck to this, and managed to keep the cost of the trip down to a reasonable level. In the end, this time, I had a glass of cider and a pizza in a typical seaside hotel restaurant.

On my map there was a road marked that ran parallel to the coast, and would take me past a waterfall that might be worth a look. This would save a long climb towards Hamilton and a return to my 80s route. In the event it didn't save much climbing, as it turned out to be a day of climbs. The map showed the road crossing over the hills towards Kawhia, with a loop towards the waterfall, and then back further along, to the Kawhia road again. After gaining a lot of height, the turnoff dropped down to the waterfall, and was then blocked off so that I had to climb back the way I came.

Forest walk

The waterfall, like others I would see later, was away from the road along an impressive forest walk. So much of NZ's forests, are unique to NZ. Every bit of vegetation seems to be worth a look.

A mixture of tough volcanic rocks over soft sedimentary rocks, and rather a lot of water constantly falling from the sky, make NZ the perfect place for spectacular waterfalls.

I headed back to the Kawhia road to find it soon turned to gravel. This was a very tough riding surface because of the extreme camber, making tough climbs tougher and descending steep drops very difficult. The particle size of the gravel, as well as the corrugated surface, made this section of road one of the most difficult of the whole trip.

The sheer joy of reaching tarmac at the road junction made the last bit of the ride into town near perfect.

Before looking for a campsite I bought a coffee and a meat pie. Meat pies are a big favourite in both Australia and NZ, making it important for me to keep testing the quality of such an important national product. Sitting on a bench outside the shop, as I tucked into my snack, crumbs from the puff pastry floated down to the ground. A flight of sparrows zoomed in and hoovered up the crumbs. I've heard that sparrows are a fairly recently introduced bird to NZ. It seems to be the perfect place for them as there are far more there than in the UK.

Whale boats

There is no shortage of campsites in Kawhia – I saw three. My legs were like jelly after the day's climbing, so I had a nap after pitching the tent. Walking into town along a pathway that ran alongside but above the beech, I could see through the trees crews practicing for the famed whaleboat race this town holds every New Years Day. It was a bit of a surprise to find that all the little cafes that had been open when I reached the town at midday were now closed. The whole town, with the exception of a small store where I did buy some food, had closed down by 4pm.

My original route had continued along route 1 from Hamilton to Lake Taupo. The plan then was to try and do a figure eight around both islands, and see as much of NZ spectacular coast as possible. The new ride had the advantage of more of the small roads having tarmac, and I had much more time to stay close to the coast. Before, I had failed to visit Cape Egmont, so this was a priority. How to get there was a problem. There were roads that ran relatively close to the coast but as these were gravel, the best option seemed to be to follow the 31 up to the 3, and follow that south and west.

Climbing along the twisting and turning 31, was at times helped by a strong wind from the sea, that gave me a push each time I headed east. Close to the top, at a rest area, just before reaching the 3, a kindly farmer asked me if I would like to spend the night at his farm. Very tempting, but I pressed on.

At a later rest area, a middle-aged man was telling me he had given up smoking. It seems he had just had a by-pass operation. I think that would put most people off smoking!

The 3, being much more of a main road, had more places to stop and get a drink or a snack. I didn't resist the temptation.

Te Kuiti had some decent fruit shops. Fruit is my main snack on a ride, and this was my chance to stock up. Just because it is more of a main road didn't mean the 3 lacked hills. Some of them were long and tough.

In a tiny town called Piopio I had my second breakfast of the day (I always try and start the day with porridge). At home, for me to have egg and bacon is now very rare, but on tour, why not once in a while? This time was very special. The bacon was the best I remember having in my life. When I'm cycling, and hungry, things frequently taste better than normal, but this bacon really was exceptional.

Where the 3 reached the coast, between the small villages of Awkino and Mokau, I camped. Being next to the sea and listening to it roar up the beach is one of my great pleasures. At this campsite it came in with a vengeance, however, for a non New Zealander, the black-sand beach along parts of the coastline, this camp being an example, always seems a bit odd.

Early morning
The 3, at times follows closely the extremely attractive coast, crossing many rivers, as it heads to a distant Mount Egmont, that can be seen long before reaching there. On some of the longer climbs there was a short tunnel, usually near the top.

A cool early morning after a rainy night was frequently followed by sunshine and, later in the day, temperature in the high twenties. This was wonderful weather as I rode along roads that carved their way through one of the most enjoyable cycling routes anywhere in the world.

Just before the little village of Urenu was a brewery with a café. It was much too early for a beer, so I had a coffee. A quick look at their advertising suggest a less sycophantic aproach to the royal family than is normal in the UK.

Approaching New Plymouth, Mt Egmont became more dominent, although it was covered in a cotton wool like clinging cloud that made it difficult to tell if it really was the mountain, or just a mountain shaped cloud.

The town of New Plymouth was a confusing mess because of major road works. This was a pity because had I been able to cross to a coastal cycle path I was to find later, I could have avoided the town and cycled directly to the campsite, which was in a splendid position, and looked down over the harbour.

After pitching the tent, a walk into town along the cycle path gave a much more pleasurable impression of the place. The next morning, a brief stop at a café, where I had a coffee with coconut sugar, became a problem. As I left the place, a quick chat with a local doctor must have broken my routine. Twenty km down the road, a man was pointing at my head. Although I thought this a bit odd, I instinctively put my hand to my head, and found my helmet missing. I am not a person who normally wears a helmet, but this is no excuse, as this was the third trip in the year where I had to wear one, and it is the law in NZ. Anyway, the result was me cycling on to the next town with a cycle shop, Opunake, and buying a cheep replacement for my far from cheep carbon fibre version, and avoiding being spotted by the police and having to pay a fine.

A bit of information I did get while having a morning coffee; on the top of Mt Egmont it had been snowing overnight. The snow like cloud had been replaced by the real stuff.

Opunake, on the top of a hill overlooking the sea, still has one of white posts used to guide in ships. In the 19th century, because of the huge number of wide rivers, travelling on the land for any distance was difficult, and boats would take people between areas of population.

A white post on the beach, lined up with the one above on the hillside, would help boats avoid the rocks.

The wind almost all the way around Cape Egmont had been helpful, and by the time I reached Wanganui I was getting used to receiving a gentle push up each climb. This was no support for my original *back wind all the way* theory because I had not been travelling on my original route. At the little village of Bulls I joined the Route 1. It was not only now possible to ride along it, but most of the time it was the only coastal route, but I was on my 80s route at last.

I'm guilty of not checking my emails very often. The campsite at Wanganui river was the ideal place to catch up with the rest of the world. It didn't quite work out as planned. A message on my iPhone informed me someone from New Zealand was trying to get into my yahoo account. While I suspected that was me, I did have a problem as couldn't remember my latest password. I was doing reasonably well at answering the questions to prove who I was, until I was asked my date of birth. Something I thought I knew, but I obviously didn't, because I was informed my answer was incorrect and I was barred from this account! Anyway, its no real hardship to do without emails for a couple of months, I'v been without them for most of my life.

Christmas was getting close

The little coastal towns along Route 1 seem to be split into two parts, one part next to the road, and one next to the beach. Foxton beach, where I camped one night, was a typical example. The little town of Foxton was adjacent to the main road with its supermarket, Dutch windmill, and cafes, but the beach with just a few houses and a campsite, was about 5km away.

Leaving Roiute 1, and onto the *Coast South Cyc;e Route,* took me away from the increasingly busy main road. I ran along a mixture of minor roads and gravel tracks which were mostly OK. Unfortunately, some of the gravel paths

Seashore from the cycle path.
swept down tight little hills and deposited me into soft sand at the bottom. However, it did give a variety of coastal views, small lakes, and coastal towns with cafes. I stopped for a coffee, and had a nutcake that was so tooth-rotting sweat the place must have been sponsored by a hard pressed local dentist. Back riding on the main road was fine while there was a wide hard shoulder. At one stage this ran out altogether and I found myself on a very narrow cyclepath, with a drop down to a stormy sea smashing into rocks on my right, and extremely busy road next to a railway line on my left. Then it started to rain. I was getting close to a campsite I had been told about earlier in the day, but the rain was now sheeting it down and my lights would have been very useful, if I still had them,

because the sky darkened, and I was back riding on the hard shoulder with cars passing me much too close for comfort. The bright light of a motel appeared on my left, and they got a customer for the night.

The ferry terminal was now only 30km away, and on a bright rain-free morning, cycling along the main road on the hard shoulder, seemed OK. However, cycles were soon directed onto a route that ran west of Route 1 (which became a motorway once again), and was only well marked in parts. With help from a fellow cyclist, I did manage to find a series of roads that ran in roughly the right direction, until I was deposited onto a cyclepath next to the motorway, not long before it joined Route 2. It was now clear the ferry was close by, and other helpful cyclist sent me westward and around a rather odd sort of cycle route to the ferry. I was in luck, the 9am ferry was late, and they got me on before it sailed.

Thirty years before, I had spent the night with my Uncle Jess and Auntie Leni in Auckland. In those days I had to go to the railway station to book my ticket. Sadly, they are no longer in the land of the living, and I was able to avoid the big city altogether.

Picton in the 80s etched such a camping memory on my brain, that it will never be forgotten. It was Christmas day, and it rained, and it rained, and it rained. My tent, was pitched on a high patch of ground, was surrounded by grass when I first looked at it from the TV room, an hour later, when I looked again it was in the middle of a lake.

Picton this time was bright, colourful and much more touristy. The Top Ten camp site I found myself on didn't look like, and in all likelyhood wasn't, the same onc I remembered. In fact, the whole town looked different, but was still a rather pleasant place to be.

Picton

The main road gently climbs around a forested mountainside, following the railway line, towards Blenheim. A pleasant following wind helped to push me up the hills and enabled the use of a higher gear on the descents.

Blenheim

Blenheim is a fairly big place with all the shops, banks, and in my case cafes, anyone could wish for. In Blenheim I met a Belgium couple I was to see later. They told me of a cycle friendly lodge on the road a little further south. The next day I did see the sign 55km south of Blenheim, next to it, it read, 'cross the railway line and continue for 1.5km' Later I was to find my friends had spent Christmas day there, and had been treated extremely well.

I was to continue through the hills, and then down to a beautiful, but still hilly, coastline, as it first came and then disappeared from view. Close to the land the sea was almost yellow, then a greeny blue, a sky blue, and on the horizon, purple.

Frequent crossing of rivers was a constant reminder of the number of bridges that had to be built before a complete road network wss possible in NZ. Some of the older ones had been left in place as a tourist interest after the new roads had been built. In the 19th century rivers often had to be forded and were only open for part of the year.

Newer roads freqently had a hard shoulder, but the roads narrowed at bridges, where a sign warns drivers of cyclists.

Sometimes these signs would light up as a cyclist rode by and stayed bright until the other side was reached.

From the bridge
It was at Waipapa Bay that I was reminded of my last trip. A fibreglass figure of a crayfish hung over a little shop next to a campsite. The shop was closed because it was Christmas day, but the campsite was open. The fibreglass figure was new, but I remembered a number of huts along the coast selling crayfish.

I decided to stay at the campsite for the night. Unlike most of the bigger places, it didn't have a microwave, a toaster, or a kettle. There was a barbeque and a gasring, and for the first time since I stayed at the old school on my first night, I had to dig out my camping pans!
One thing Waipapa Bay did have was bird life. Over the railway line, on little coastal rock formations, birds spiralled upwards by the millions

The next morning I was riding along a stunning rocky coastline. It was very easy to miss, unless I stopped and looked for movement below, but once I did, I found the rocks were covered with fantastically well camaflouged seals. There were mothers feeding their young, and at the same time dominant males were engaged in an all-out war. Looking now, my pictures of the seals on the rocks show, well, just rocks.

An attempt to pick out the seals resulted in almost total failure. Further along the coast, when I nipped behind a bush for a pee, a huge male objected strongly to my presence. He was having a nap in the shade. I backed away and found another spot.

This wonderful coastline continues to Kaikoura, where the Kaikoura peninsula sticks out into the ocean. Near its tip is an old whaling house.

Old whaling station

Robert Fyffe established a whaling station here in 1842, but long before that, 800 to 1,000 years ago, it was a moa-hunter settlement (the now extinct large flightless bird – an egg found here was 178mm in diameter and 240mm long), and crayfish was, and still is, a key industry. Kaikaura means 'to eat crayfish' in Maori. It was a place I didn't take much notice of on my first trip, and neither did Capt Cook when he stopped here in 1770. Now things are very different, this small fishing village has turned itself into a whale watching (instead of killing) and swimming with dolphins centre. Near the entrance to the town centre were pictures of devastating floods that took place in the not too distant past, mostly around the Christmas period. I was there on boxing day!

Winding, climbing and going through an occasional tunnel, the road heads into more open countryside, away from the coast but not the traffic. Lots of people seemed to be heading home after the Christmas break, many taking their boats on trailers with them. Bends were frequently very tight, some had 25kph speed restrictions. For the first time on this trip I was capable of breaking the speed limit, but decided not to. Away from the coast was the open countryside with the more traditional view of NZ farmland.

A small house by the roadside gave a real view of rural tradition. Its one room interior gave the cramped reality of 19th century living.

At Cheviot there is a sign to Gore Bay, and it is close to the famed Cathedral Cliffs. My legs had just the right amount of exercise for the day without a diversion, so I wasn't tempted.

As the main road (route 1) headed further south and a little further from the coast, finding a campsite meant riding to little coastal towns along roads without an exit. Waikuku was one of these places.

When I was charged much more than usual, and given a worse than normal place to pitch the tent, I did complain and get myself a better patch of grass, but didn't feel inclined to leave, cycle back up to the main road again, and then down to another coastal village. Anyway, I suppose I was being spoiled by the shear quality and good value of the average campsite in NZ.

My approach to Christchurch, like other major cities, had me directed along a road than ran parallel to the now motorway.

Unlike most other places where this happened, I was not directed up into the hills, the west side of Christchurch is dead flat. There are not many places in NZ where that's the case. The town centre is a very sad place.

While I am sure they are doing one hell of a lot of work to put the place right, there are also arguments going on about what should be restored and what should be knocked down and rebuilt.

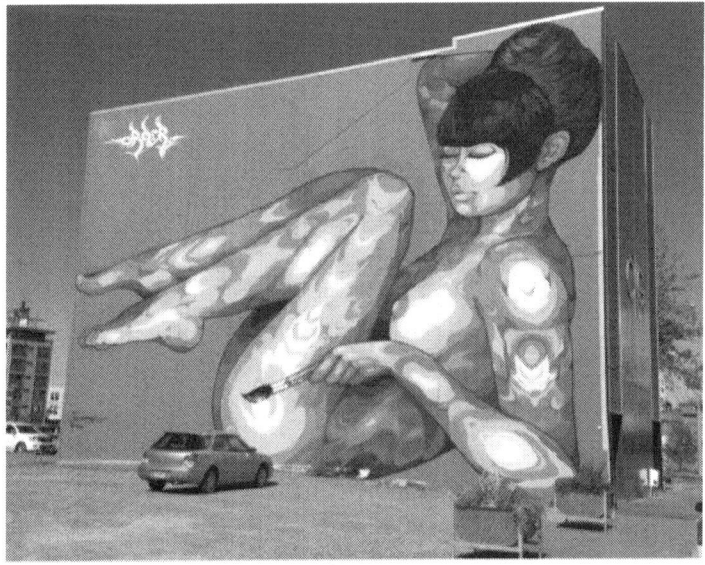

Graffiti on a grand scale!

35

This is very much the case with the cathedral which was the centre piece of the city. The restoration has been costed, but many of the church authorities want a totally new building. Before I left NZ, on St Valantines Day, another great earthquake hit the city, this time, thankfully, without killing anyone.

Away from the city, was also away from the motorway, and unfortunately away from several days of gentle back winds. Overcast sky and drizzle didn't produce the most desirable cycling conditions. Later the wind came back, and once again it was pushing me along at a decent pace. Small towns tended to give hints to what the place offered.

Salmon fishing is very big in NZ, and it is not for just the extremely rich who own or rent a bit of river to the exclusion of everyone else, as it is in the UK. People from all walks of life fish for salmon – and its legal!

Home made salmon smoker
At one mid morning stop at Oran there was a statue to recognize the part blacksmiths had played in the development of NZ. Just as during the industrial revolution in the UK, it wasn't just the people with money and big ideas that developed the country, it required people with practical skills to make things work.

Timara is a much bigger place than it looks on the map, and oddly I don't remember much about it from my first trip, when I seem to have missed its impressive sea-front path overlooking the beach. For a seaside resort it also has several sporting bids for fame: Robert Fitzsimmons, a blacksmith who became a world boxing champion three times: middleweight 1891, heavyweight 1897, and light heavyweight in 1903. Dr John Lovelock was the world record holder for the mile. He also won gold in the Berlin Olympics 1500metres, where he broke the world record for that distance too. Hitler presented him with an oak tree that was planted in the grounds of the boys high school – I'm told it is still there. To top it all, they also had a race horse, Phar Lap, in the late 1920s, that travelled around the world beating all before it. He was poisoned after winning the then richest race in the world in Mexico. Seems he was a bit too good!

After riding for a while on what turned out to be the flattest part of NZ, Timara suddenly re-introduced the hills with a vengence, in the town centre.

Over the newyear period, the police were out in force stopping car after car.

I took the chance to follow smaller roads that looped out from the main road and ran closer to the coast. Alongside traffic free well-surfaced roads people were fishing from the cliffs.

Usually, due to a river having to be crossed, the minor road would head back to the major one, then loop back to the truly splendid coastline once more. The salty smell, almost the taste of the coast, was evident along these smaller roads, and was totally absent along the traffic ridden main route.

I had just reached the main road again when I saw a sign for the campsite at Hampden; headed downhill, over a railway line, and into the campground.

It was from here I was to wander along the beach, with a cliff face on my right, and the oncoming sea on my left, to find the famed Moeraki Boulders.

Inside the crystaline structure

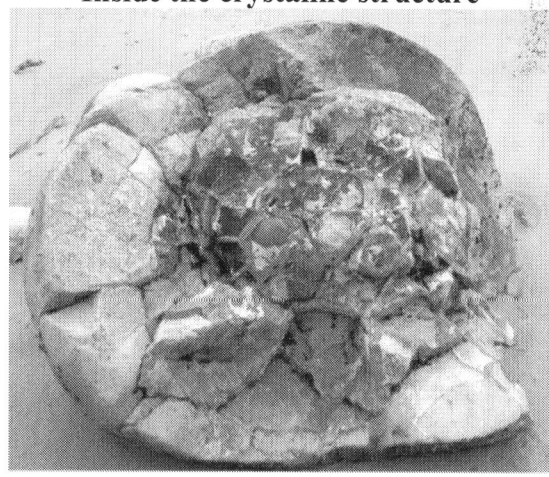

These things, like huge cannon balls were eroded from the mudstone cliffs. Minerals crystalize equally in all directions, get a layer of mudstone, before rolling down onto the beach.

As I got closer to Dunedin the coastal route remained stunningly beautiful, but at the same time, became much more hilly.

Mudstone cliffs

Although it followed the railway line, at times the road was a long way below it, at others it climbed well above. This criss crossing of the railway made it a leg testing morning.

Above the railway

Closer still to Dunedin, a cycle route was marked off to the left, over a not very encouraging Mt Cargill. By this time the legs had experienced enough climbing for one day, so I ignored it. This was a mistake. After continuing climbing for a while along the main road it turned into a motorway. Now I had a choice: either turn right along a gravel road that would take me into Dunedin on gravel all the way, or left on a gravel road that would join the tarmac of Mt Cargill. As it started to rain I headed up the gravel to Mt Cargill.

Halfway down.
The first bit was horrible, once on the tarmac it was just steady climbing in a low gear up a long, long, climb into a gale force wind. Peering through the rain at the top was, what in good conditions, would have been a great view of the harbour below in the distance. The descent was fast, slippery and cold, getting me rapidly into the city, keen to find a campsite, put up the tent and have a hot drink and some food. Fortunately, this is what happened.
Leaving Dunedin last time, I can remember riding along a tiny coastal road next to the sea, and wandering through English sounding villages, one of which was Brighton.

Although I aimed to do the same again I found myself following a marked cycle route which sort of followed highway 1. It did seem to climb up and down a good deal more than the main road, before wandering around for a good bit, then suddenly ending. I then found myself once more the main road again, as by now it was no longer a motorway. Midmorning I reached the little village of Titri, where I had a coffee and a pie. There was a campsite by a lake, and would have been a good place to stop had it been a bit later in the day. My main memory of the place was the sign as I came into town. There are many different signs to discourage motorists from speeding, this one said: **No Hospital. No Doctor. One Graveyard.**

Up to this point on the South Island I had ridden close to my 80's route, but now with the greater number of sealed roads, I could stay much closer to the coast than last time and move away from Route 1, and go through the Catlins.

Along the road I rode past a sod house. Once common in country areas everywhere, this must have been the ideal way to build a house in NZ at a time in the 19th century when almost everything was imported from the UK. Building with sods of earth would incur minimal cost, perfect for the immigrant with little money.

Sod house

Catlins

My first campsite after moving away from the main road was at Owaka. It was low cost like Europe, and also like Europe, there was no kitchen, so out came my stove and pans.

The next day took me to a very special place, Porpoise Bay.

Before reaching there I visited another waterfall, again along a walking trail that offered options of longer forest walks along what had once been a railway line.

Forest trail

This time there were options of sites to take photographs from. I rather wished I hadn't climbed to the top, as it gave my knees hell, and worse still, the photograph was no better.

Matai Falls

At the top of a hill, before dropping down to Curio Bay, I stopped at a concrete watering trough dated around 1890. It was there to ensure the team of horses that had dragged a wagon up this bloody great hill had a well-earned drink when they got to the top. However, it seems the horses had an even bigger problem on the way down when brakes were known to fail. Fortunately, my brakes are pretty good, and I descended the hill to Curio Bay, and found myself at an astonishing campsite.

Porpoise Bay Campsite consists of a small store with all the basics, a tiny kitchen, novel toilets and showers, and a wide range of places to pitch the tent.

One of many campsites.

If that was it, it would be a decent enough place to stay the night. But there is more. Much, much more. The place is surrounded by a raging wild sea. Looking out in every direction I was rewarded with the most fantastic view imaginable. I did't, but had I got myself a surf board, I could have paddled out into the sea to be surrounded by, Hector's dolphins that come in close with their young, and the yellow-eyed penguins might also have paid me a visit.

Sea washing over a fossil forest.

Looking West
Looking in a different direction I was able to see the petrified stumps of the most extensive fossil forest in the world, that dates back 160 million years.

View North West
I've been lucky enough to camp in some of the worlds most fantastic campsites. When asked, I've always said that the campsite in Uganda overlooking the Victoria Nile is the best I can think of.

Porpoise Bay has got to be up there in the same class. Sadly, the campsite on the Nile may soon disappear; a hydroelectric plant is being built. I was saddened to hear that the Porpoise Bay campsite may have to move in order to build a tourist attraction of some kind! While I can understand Uganda's desire for electricity, NZ already has lots of wonderful places for tourists, and too many can destroy the natural beauty of the place which must be its biggest selling point.

Before leaving Curio bay I spent some time having a look around the fossilised forest. There is a platform to get an overall view, and steps go down to get a closer look, providing the tide is out.

Jurassic log pile

Rather than climb up to the main road again, I decided to follow the coast around on a not too wonderful gravel road, and try and reach Slope Point, the furthest point south on the NZ mainland. It wasn't too bad on coastal road, but the spur down towards the Point had some hairy downhills.

Cliff edge, Slope Piont.
The last bit was about 2km of grass field to walk over, where I made myself most unpopular with the sheep. There seemed to be thousands of them, and they all made a dash for it when they saw me walking across their field.

After getting back to the coastal road again it was only about 6 or 7km before I hit the tarmac again, and I soon seemed to reached the small village of Fortrose, and a little store. A pie and coffee restored me almost to top form. This place once had an important past during the days of the whaling industry, and like many places along NZ rugged coast, it had its major shipwrecks too.

Tarmac again

Right on the edge of Invercargil I found a decent campsite, had a shower to rid myself of the dust from the gravel road, and cooked myself the rest of the food from my pannier. The next morning the rain was sheeting down, and there was a horrible gusting wind. I had to make a move because I had run out of food, so I headed for the town centre. After getting soaking wet, and stocking up in a supermarket, I found a Backpacker's Hotel that was also a restaurant and information centre. While I was enjoying a huge breakfast, they looked up details of campsites for my onward journey. Everything looked good, except for the rain. Then, on the TV there was a weather forecast – Invercargill was going to be dire for several days. But it looked very local. After 10km of being bashed about by the wind and rain, the rain stopped, but not the wind.

I reached Lumsden campsite with a problem. My *Continental Touring Plus* rear tyre, which had already lasted a long ride in Sweden before setting foot in NZ, was really showing signs of wear, and after the previous days gravel roads would have to be swapped with the *Schwalbe Marathon Supreme* on the front wheel, that had been new at the start of the ride. Not normally a problem. With my bent front forks it was a different story. Taking a piece of wood, cutting it to length, and notching either end, I was able to force open the fork and remove the wheel. After changing the tyres around, and with the help of several guys from around the campsite, we managed to spring the forks and get the wheel back in.

Once the tent was up, I took my first (and last) selfy, noting that I was only a shadow of my former self.

A new cycle path was opening, and was heading north. This seemed to be ideal, but it was a very new cycle path that wanted both a few thousand cyclists to ride over it to consolidate the surface, and the signposting to be sorted out. The *round the mountains cycle route,* as it is called, is a great idea. The part of it I was riding on follows the route of the old railway that ran parallel to the road; another part of it swings around further west and should include using boats on the river. It seems this bit is in trouble. There is a dispute with fishermen for some odd reason I didn't't quite understand.

Back on the road, and still heading due north, this could have been a challanging ride, but with the wind now from the south, I was riding the hills with ease. Alongside Lake Wakatipu, now just an empty road, there were signs of a vanished population, such as the site of an old school by the roadside.

The temptation was to ride all the way into Queenstown, but I didn't. By stopping at the campsite in Frankton, I could spend some time the next day wandering down the little gravel cycle route that runs alongside the Lake into Queenstown.

This was the closest I had to a rest day, the same campsite for two nights. It was an interesting stop as I met people from my home area of Derbyshire and South Yorkshire, including a student who went to the school where I used to teach (but not in the same time frame).

Queenstown is a busy town in an area of outstanding beauty, but it is the ride alongside the lake that is the real star attraction. I was now starting to see many more cyclists including several at my Frankton campsite.

From cyclepath.

Boats in Queenstown

57

Frankton really does feel like the middle of a huge mountain range. Even a visit to the supermarket has some of NZ great ski runs soaring above.

58

Heading north from here, I did have a choice, either due north over what might be a part gravel mountain road to Wanaka, or the 6, which circles around the mountains and follows a river gorge.

I was pleased I chose the 6 as there was one area of interest after another: From a bridge, high above the gorge, one bungee jumper then another would cast themselves off. The road was clinging to a mountain side which had been hacked away to produce just enough room for traffic, and leaving a high-shear cliff on one side, and a long, deep drop to the river on the other .

Bungee jumpers leap from the white centre part of the bridge to the bottom of the gorge a long way below.

Further along, a group of people with only a wetsuit, fins and a board, were drifting on mass through the white water of, what looked to me, a dangerous fast flowing river.

Whitewater travel!

Almost hidden from view, dug into the hillside were old gold mines.

On a hillside was the site of an old gold mine, now a tourist attraction. It reminded me that on my last trip, when, not all that far away from this spot, there was a campsite sign which read, *Camping and Goldpanning*. Paying my way by gold panning unfortunately didn't work out!

When I stopped at Cromwell, I found that shortly after I had ridden through the gorge, it was closed. The fire brigade had to be called out. It seems the fire was started when a wheel on a caravan caught fire.
Still, mostly with a back wind, I was finding the 6 a very pleasant route to follow.

The next morning, clouds were clinging to the mountains.

Before following the 6 to Lake Hawea, I dropped down into Wanaka just to see what I had missed by not taking the mountain route. It was a pleasant enough little town, but I still felt I had taken the best option.

Above from the campsite

Mountains beyond

There is a lakeside campsite at the south end of Lake Hawea with a wonderful view of the lake.

When the ice sheets carved out the valley for Lake Hawea, they also carved out a parallel valley for the equally beautiful Lake Wanaka. The 6 manages to climb alongside both lakes by swapping over from Hawea to Wanaka, and providing a stunning cycle ride, enjoyed by quite a few cyclists on the day I rode along there.

First Hawea and then Wanaka.

Beyond the lakes I was determined to find a campsite before crossing the Haast Pass.

Snow capped mountains

The small village of Makrova is spread over several kilometers with lots of distance and almost no content.

However, at the south end, there is a filling station and a café, with around the back, a campsite. I was to find, the next day, a similar setup at the other end, about 4km further on.

Anyway, this first campsite was an excellent small place with everything I required, and I was able to pitch the tent in an orchard away from some of the gale force wind that was just starting to become a problem.

Moments after pitching the tent, a hedgehog wandered by. Only the second of the trip.

There are only two climbs I really remember from my 80s tour, and one of them was the Haast Pass. Although it had been opened in the 1960s it was still regarded as a tough route in the 80s. It wasn't because it was then a gravel road, for me the difficult part was the corrugations from struggling cars on the corners, that made it memorable. This time there was tarmac all the way. As I climbed closer and closer to the pass's top, the trees that gave shelter at the start of the climb got less and less, and there was more and more rain, and to top it all, a gale force headwind.

For the climb, my clothing was about right - The usual cycle vest and shorts with a waterproof jacket.

The heavy rain on the top was joined with hail, making it both cold and slippery. For a long descent of a mountain pass it is wise to put on extra clothing. This wasn't an option. Had I opened a pannier all my spare clothing would be soaked too.

As a one time cyclo-cross rider, difficult riding conditions are normal. But, this was one hell of a hairy ride for the first bit: wet, icy, very steep-roads, with tight bends where hard braking was essential. The ideal of only using the back brake in icy conditions – a back wheel skid is not a problem, a front one is – wasn't an option as the road was too steep. All I could do was brake hard in a straight line before the bend, then soar around without using brakes. Away from the top of the pass it became much less steep, and I was able to follow the River Haast down very quickly, only slowed each time I reached a one-car-width road bridge, the priorities of which were all against downhill traffic, and called for more heavy braking.

This was a very cold descent, and by Haast I was frozen to the bone, and stopped at the only open café for a hot drink and some food. It was full of people all sheltering from the rain, so by the time I got a hot drink I found it difficult to hold the mug.

Open, wet, windy campsite.

Once at the campsite, putting up the tent would have made an interesting video, had I not been alone in a gale swept field. My normal practice in the wind is: first put in one peg to anker down the tail end tent, before letting it line itself up with the tail end into the wind.

Then I put in the pole, then the other pegs. I did almost get the pole in place before the gale force wind pulled out the peg – along with a great sod of earth – and dragged me and the tent almost off the ground and across the field! Once the hang-gliding experiment was over, I found a huge rock to hold the end peg in place while the tent was erected.

SW Coast

Almost the whole of the east side of South Island, with the exception of the extreme south, had been hot sunshine with little rain. All of this was to change as I cycled north on the west coast.

After cycling for about 60km in fairly miserable conditions, a break and a hot drink were wanted, but this part of the coast is remote. I had ridden past a pleasant enough campsite, where I could have paid by putting my money in an honesty envelope, but it was still early and I wanted to press on a bit.

Looking down from a long bridge I could see a café. It was part of a salmon farm. It was also the only place for miles around where a coffee and a snack were available, so was full of cyclists, most of whom were, with their cake and drinks, peering over the balcony to look at the tanks of salmon below.

Overcast, windy and wet.
It was still quite a long way to Fox Glacier, the next place on the map likely to have a campsite, when I saw a motel.

There was also a camp sign, but on the door of the office was a sign: **Back at 4pm.**
But for a German couple telling me what a pleasant place it was, I would have pressed on to Fox. I am so glad I did stay as I had a great time there and met all sorts of interesting people. The place was called Hunt's Beach.

Fox Glacier, on a tour around NZ, isn't the sort of place to miss. The climbs on this short stretch should have been tough, but with a powerful wind behind, were no problem.

There is a turn-off to the glaciers before the town centre, but I had little desire to visit dripping ice in the unpleasant rainy conditions that morning. Instead, headed into town and had a second breakfast, egg and bacon. The first time for several days.

It rained all afternoon and all night, so not a good day for looking either at the mountains or the glaciers.

Low cloud slowly drifts away.

At first sight when I glanced at the map, 25km to the next glacier at Franz Josef, looked hardly worth getting the bike out for. The distance was very deceptive; there is one hell of a lump of rock to get over between the two glaciers, and a morning of steep climbs and winding descents.

Helicopters - down in bad weather.

As I cycled away from Fox the clouds, bit by bit, started to lift. Nevertheless, the helicopters, used to take people up to the glaciers looked as if they were going to have a quiet day. Half way down the long descent into Franz Josef, a woman cyclist climbing towards me, shouted, "You have a long, long descent ahead!" I had to inform her that there was still a long, long climb to go for her.

Whataroab is well known for its White Heron. What I remember it for, is a little café where they dug out a plastic chair for me when, dripping with water, I came in for a hot drink and a snack. Opposite the café was a sheltered seating area where I parked my bike and put on an extra cycle vest. It was not just a wet morning, it was bloody cold one too.

Up to this point the day's ride had been almost flat – a rare thing in NZ – but it didn't last all morning. A large group of soaking-wet cyclists were heading to Franz Josef on stripped down bikes. Their luggage was following behind in a van. I was pleased I could get at my extra clothing when I wanted it.

Mémorial Park

I spent the night at Harihari Backpackers. This little towns bid for fame is it being the landing spot for the first solo flight from Australia. The whole thing was an outrageous adventure. Flights of this type were forbidden in Australia, so Guy Menzies lied about his destination and set off for NZ without informing anyone.

The landing didn't quite work out as planned either, with him being dumped upside down in the mud. Guy had many more adventures before, like lots of other Australians and New Zealanders, being killed in WWII. There is a memorial park in the village. The town has trees with plaques, to what I think is the memory of those killed in the war.

Misty Lake Lanthe
It was a dank, miserable day as I cycled passed Lake Lanthe, which was hidden, in mist. I did make an attempt to photograph it when the mist lifted a little.

There is no doubt what the town of Ross stands for. Like many towns along this coast it owes its existence to gold. Ross, however, has a better claim than most, not only are they still mining it there, but it is the site of NZs largest nugget. In 1907, a nugget of 99 ounces, to be known as ***Honourable Rodney,*** was found there. I hit a different type of gold. Just as I was starting to feel really hungry I found a place selling eggs and bacon. I sat outside the café chatting to a guy who was wandering around NZ fly-fishing for salmon. Shortly afterwards I met an American couple who were trying to follow a cycle trail.

The rain stopped, the wind was pushing from behind, as I sped towards Hokitika. On a long climb I was charging up using a big gear, suddenly feeling I had dropped 20 years, I caught a guy who was finding the climb difficult, no doubt his problem was the huge back pack that was weighing him down.

On the way into town, on the left before crossing the bridge, is the site of a pre-war commercial airline: The south Westland Air Service, now almost nothing remains.
I thought I would quickly find a campsite in Hokitika, but ended up at the *Beach-side Holiday Park*, a place that doesn't cater for tents, but they let me put up mine anyway, right next to the kitchen and toilet block.

The South Westland Air Service – the way it used to be.

As I am someone who has spent some time wandering around NZ, and had never seen a Kiwi, in Hokitika I felt the urge to put things right. There is a centre, very much a child centered place, where among several other rare indigenous species, there are kiwi. On mainland NZ they have all but disappeared, and being nocturnal would be difficult to see in the wild anyway, so a Kiwi Centre was the only chance I was going to get. The place was suitably quiet, almost dark, with a real looking forest floor. The kiwi I was watching was about the size of a large chicken, but with of course a very different shape and totally different feathers and feet. It moved around quickly, rooting with its beak in the floor detritus. Very interesting, and not quite what I expected!

Heading in the direction of Greymouth along an almost flat road, occasional gravel cycle path, and a recent clip on cycle bridge, resulted in a quick ride to the biggest town for some time.

Not such a crap morning

Clip on cycle path

Before reaching the town centre I saw two campsites on the left. After a visit to the bank, although less than 50km had been covered, I decided not to go on.

Seaside cycle path

The route ahead looked wild and empty and I didn't want to have to do a huge ride before finding a place to stop. As luck would have it, the next day I found a couple of campsites about 10km north of the city. But, I headed back to the south of town and the closest campsite, which turned out to be a great place next to the coastal cycle route and the beach. After putting up the tent I was surrounded by tame 'wild' rabbits!

It might have been almost flat just south of Greymouth, but the coast road north is not. This was a mining area, not gold like Ross, these people mined and lost their lives for coal. When the mines were open, large tight communities thrived. In one village there were two international Rugby League players, as well as top-level sports people of every kind, but now there were only ghosts of former times.

A monument to 1967 mining disaster
For the cycle tourist, this route is outstanding. NZ has many stunning views and wonderful coastlines, and this northern coast stands out even from that high standard.
Every bend of the road, every climb – and there are many – provide another fantastic view of the sea.

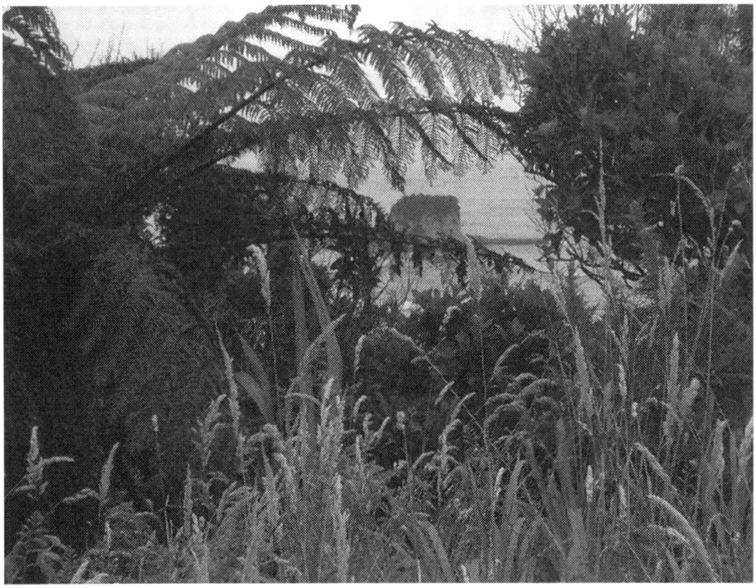

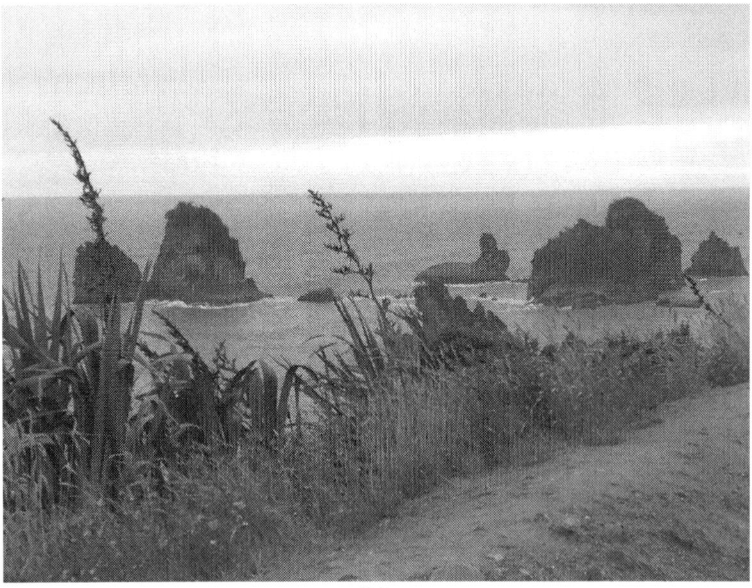

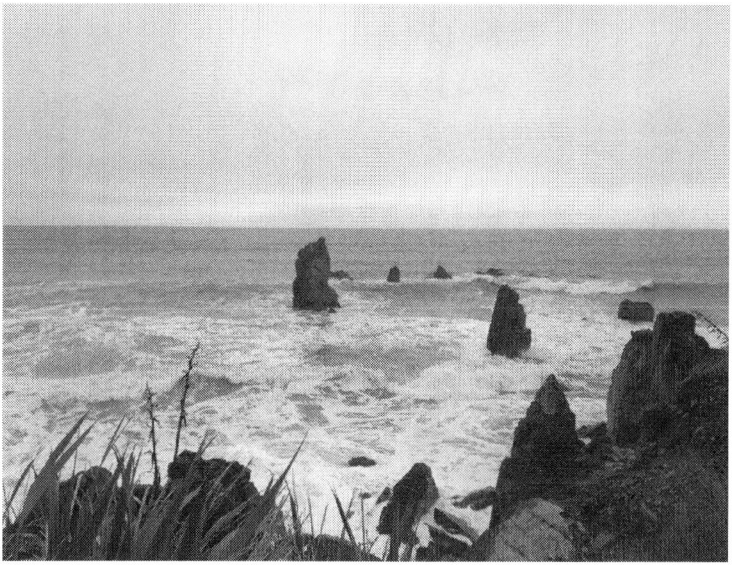

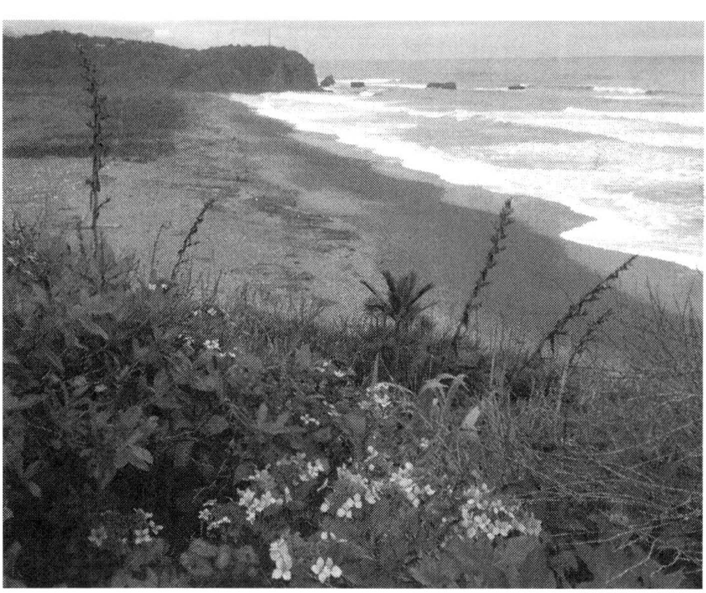

I camped at Punakaiki, and could not have found a better place. At the top of the hill is a marked out route around the very unusual *pancake rocks and blowholes.*

Pancake rocks – odd rock layers

Blowholes

The way the sedimentary rock has been deposited in piles of sandwich like formations, I am told, is very rare.

The blowholes, where the sea has eroded rocks, forming caves and inlets, shoot water into the air when the tide is right – it wasn't for me.

Inlet above and Punakaiki Cavern below

Halfway down the hill is an attractive cavern. It had been raining and was very slippery, and with my dodgy knees, didn't go too far in.
Down at the bottom of the hill, beyond the campsite, is a bridge from where long river walks start. This is the sort of town where I could spend a week and still find things to do. I didn't, and pressed on the next day.

The wonderful coastline continues until Charelston.

The now tiny town of Charleston was once a huge place with pubs noted for raucous behaviour was an area of decadent living, cantered around gold mining. When I rode into the place the first thing I saw was a great structure on the right. It is a café and base for *'Underworld Rafting'*.

I didn't take part as booking ahead is required. It seems to be a raft and railway trip along a great cavern system. In the café, above all this rafting, I attempted to get a coffee, but they had run out of water!

In Charleston I met a couple that had planned to stay at the Charleston campsite the previous night, but because they had spent so long looking at the pancake rocks and the blowholes, stayed at Punakaiki.

They were telling me how pleased they were that they didn't go on. It had been a tough morning of climbing, and would have been very tough at the end of a days cycling. After Charleston, the road moved away from the coast and there was only one really tough climb, then an easy ride into Westport.
Just out of town there is a chance to see an old gold mine.

Westport, like several NZ towns, is spread out. It is a fairly big town, but covers the area of a city, and the campsite is away from the town centre. Outside the supermarket was a touring bike with dropped handlebars and a fitting for its Rohloff gear on the drops – just like I used to use. I didn't see the owner, but I suspected a Brit.

From Westport the 6 heads NE along the Buller Gorge. There is a very interesting café/campsite after 35km called Berlins.

Covering the walls are pictures of the disastrous earthquake damage, when the place was totally cut off. From an earlier time, there is a letter from the chief surveyor complaining that he couldn't't keep his workforce as they kept finding gold and packing up work. Problems, problems! When the road was completed, it was very, very narrow. There is a picture of a small horse drawn vehicle with one wheel rubbing the cliff face, and the other on the edge of a drop down to the river way below.

Another little town, Inangahua, has a museum dedicated to the people killed in endless, year after year, earthquakes.

Alongside pictures of huge structural damage there are human stories of those who died or went missing, never to be found.

Further along the river, where a long suspension bridge is a big attraction, I found a faded mark on the road indicating the fault line for one of these great earth movements.

The Buller Gorge road follows the winding river.

The campsite at Merchinson is alongside the river in an ideal spot. I spent the afternoon on a sheltered platform on the riverbank reading, while people below dived into the water.

The Gowan Bridge Store, affectionately known as "Dizzy's Store" was first erected at Pikomanu to serve the railway families who were constructing the railway line from Nelson to Inangahua Junction. In 1926 the store was relocated to Gowan Bridge and re-erected by Percy and Ralph Diserens without much extra help. It was expected to follow and serve the construction workers, but when the railway building ceased the store remained and served the local community. After Percy Diserens retired the store was run by his son Ralph. In 1977 the store was wound up with an eight-hour continuous auction. Both father and son were known as Dizzy.

Just when a snack would help, there was a sign to say there was a store here for many years. There was also an airfield, and a railway station – all gone.

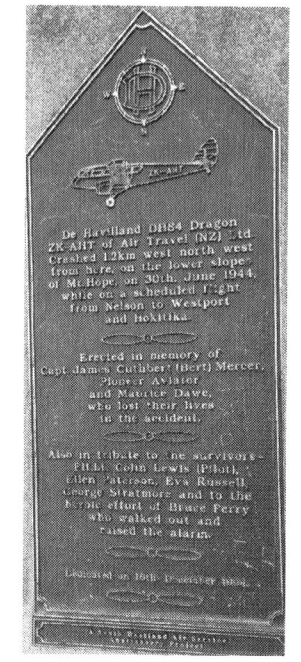

An old railway station is also the site of a basic camping spot. I wasn't tempted; the place seemed to have more than its fair share of sand flies. This was, however, a very interesting place with its history described in both photographs and text. At the turn of the last century excursion trains would take a thousand passengers at a time down to Richmond. Next to this site, a 185m railway tunnel was built through a granite spur in the 1920s, as part of the lines continual expansion. By 1954, it was all over for the railway, and the last train ran. Now, there is no railway line, no town, no people, just a very basic campsite.

Just beyond this point, after a morning of mostly climbing in mostly dry conditions, I was treated to some very easy, mostly downhill, riding. Ahead was a road junction, and I could either continue to follow the 6 all the way to Nelson, or take a smaller road due north to the coast. Just before the junction, first there was a motor vehicle accident and a woman unfortunately received what looked like a broken arm – as there was plenty of help I didn't't stop – and then there was a campsite called Quinney's Bush. A different sort of place from the average campsite. It had once been a children's play area, and in effect still was, but was now also a campsite. It was a good place to stop before making up my mind which way to go.

Soon after putting up the tent it started to rain again leaving me with the problem of drying my towel after showering. A walk to the other end of this rather large campground gave me the ideal solution. A sheltered area had a wood-burning stove and a washing line – this could't have been more perfect.

One huge play area

Plenty of useful information in the toilet block!

I decided to head north on the smaller road. It would take longer to Nelson, but with much more of the coastline to ride along. After having ridden only a short distance on this new road it was clear it was a good choice.

Riding beyond a campsite that claimed to be the best in the region – I didn't look to find out – I found myself in nut growing area, also with lots of fruit trees. Avoiding the fruit and nut case jokes, I rapidly descended to the coast and into the quite large seaside resort of Motueka. It was a good place to stock up with food in the supermarket.

Riding along the coast in dire weather isn't the best way to see it at its best.
There was a cycle trail, but early on I didn't use it, seeing no sense in splashing through the mud. Once beyond Richmond the cycle route then became a better option and I followed it all the way into Nelson.
The campsite I ended up at, after wandering around the town, was on the south edge of the town, beyond a complex of road works, without signs, and with only a very small space for tents. We all pitched together on a small patch of grass.

In the morning the weather was horrible. For the first time on the trip I didn't get up early. Later than usual, I managed to find a dry place in the kitchen, while making my porridge and coffee, then sat in the TV room for a while it sheeted it down outside. It was 10am before I set off into town, had poached eggs and bacon for a second breakfast before getting moving.

Wet!

The coastal road is flat, with a cycle path running alongside for a short distance out of Nelson, and then the cycle path stops and not long afterwards, it starts to climb. It stopped raining so I had a good look at the map, it looked like a hilly day. While I was map reading, two young women from Sydney, Poppy and Rada, cycled by.

Shortly afterwards I past them on this long, long climb, and I was to meet them again at the campsite. Their description of finding the first climb tough, then after a long descent, the second climb even tougher, then another long descent, before the third climb. This last climb, they felt, didn't bother them so much, as by then they were used to continual climbing. I had to agree with them. I had ridden less than 60km, but it was a tough day's ride.

The three of us, along with lots of other people, ended up at the Pelorus Bridge Campsite. After pitching my tent alongside a stream, I had a wander around some of the fabulous walks marked out around the campsite. Chatting to a Kiwi guy called Kim, we both had a look at some of the huge trees. As well as the size, it was also the distance from the ground before the lowest branches that was so impressive. Not easy trees to climb!

It was a bit too early in the morning when I reached Havelock to give the famed Havelock Green Mussels their due consideration, tempting as it might be. Instead of a flat white coffee and steak pie I sometimes had for mid-morning, I had mussel pie with my coffee. A token, but worthwhile snack, as it was rather good.

Outside the museum is an old (1893) locomotive built in Glasgow. Nothing too striking about that, Glasgow built hundreds of locomotives that were exported around the world. What was different about this one was it was used to haul timber, found to be not that good for that purpose, and was then given a number of other roles during its very long active life.

The 6 continues all the way to Blenheim, but I wanted to follow the small road to Picton via Queen Charlotte Sound. In December 1773, Queen Charlotte Sound was to have been the rendezvous point for Capt Cook's ship the *Resolution* and Capt Furneaux's ship *Adventure*. They failed to meet, and Cook left before the *Adventure* arrived. Furneaux sent some of his men out to find fresh food. They were invited to dinner by a local tribe – and ended up as the main course! Cannibalism was common across the Pacific region at that time.

Logs for export

Dropping down from the hillside and into Picton, I saw the booking office for the ferry to North Island was on my left.

I booked a ticket for the next day, followed the camping signs that I took to be for a different campsite from last time, but ended up at the same site.

I was at the ferry terminal at 7am and was on the boat not long after for the 8am start. Quite a contrast to my ferry ride in the opposite direction.

Getting off the ferry, and on to the cycle path next to the road, was still a bit messy, but I was soon on my way as the ferry was in Wellington by 11.30. I did not intend to ride far, just get out of the Wellington area. The contrast from the South Island was an unpleasant shock, not just the traffic, but everything seemed to be rushing around, after weeks of gentle riding.

Route 2 took me all the way to Lower Hutt where I was sure there was a campsite. It turned out to be away from the main road, to the south of town, and I found myself camped by some bushes, on the edge of a large field. As well as it not being a very friendly place, they charged me about twice what I had been paying. It did have one redeeming feature; in the TV room I was able to watch a rugby 7s tournament for the whole afternoon.

The cycle path towards Upper Hutt wasn't difficult to find as it is very close to the campsite. It was such a pleasant change from the previous day. At first, it was a ride along the Hutt River on a tarmac path.

The cycle path started with good tarmac

After a while the cycle path did turn to gravel, but they do seem to be still working on this route and, one day I suspect, it will be tarmac much further along the river.
For a while, while there were workmen below, I rode along a small pathway on the banking, where I said, "Good Morning" to a gentleman of my generation.

In reply, he said, "Where is your bell?"

He was convinced that everyone should still have a bell on their bike, just as it was when he was a teenager in Essex. As I pointed out to him, although most people do have bells on touring bikes in Germany, and it is quite a good idea where walkers and cyclists are using the same track, I rarely do, and would much rather stop and speak than charge by ringing my bell.

Rimutaka Hill was one of the few hills I remember from my last trip. It turned out to be a bit of a surprise then, and caught me out again this time, for a different reason. I had a puncture.

There was no penetration of the tyre, it was a pinch puncture, caused by me not having enough air in my tyres, and it was my fault. After changing the tyre around down the south of South Island, I pumped up the tyre has hard as I could. The plan had been to get to a big town with a cycle shop, and use a proper pump with a gauge, but I kept forgetting, although once in a while I would pump in a little extra air. I had help from a man in a nearby house to find the double hole - the traffic on the 2 was so loud I couldn't'hear where the air was coming from. With two small patches in place, I set off again. 10km on the tyre went down again, one patch had lifted in the baking hot sunshine. My spare inner tube, that seemed fine before I left home, had a valve that no longer worked, so I put a big patch over the two small ones.

This long, long climb has an historical interest to New Zealanders. After a tough training course at a huge military camp in Featherston, the soldiers would walk over Rimutaka Hill to catch their boat to WWI. For quite a few of them it was their last long look at their homeland.,

Featherston no longer has a huge army camp, its now quite a small place, and I was concerned that I might not find a campsite. Luckily, on the right as I entered the little town was a motel with camping, and after Lower Hutt, more normal prices again.

While I was packing some muslie bars into my handlebar bag, a little girl came over to watch me pack. She said she liked muslie bars, and as she dashed off after I past one over to her, she then had second thoughts. Stopped, and came back and said, "My brother likes muslie bars." Seemed like a good sister to have!

Masterton, being the first big place, and having a good cycle shop, was my chance to get the pressure in my tyres checked after the puncture. Despite me thinking I had put enough air in after the repair, both tyres were well below the correct pressure. The correct tyre pressure and a back wind, had the bike floating along as in a dream, only spoiled by road repairs and sticky tarmac.

Approaching Eketahuna was another Kiwi centre, this time with a white Kiwi advertised. I didn't stop there, but I did stop in the town, and saw a sign for a campsite.

The campsite was about 2km away from the main road, almost around the back of the town, and down a short steep hill. It turned out to be a very pleasant, extremely good value, interesting place. I pitched the tent and washed my dirty clothes and stuck things out to dry in the hot sunshine.

Woodville is at the junction of the road to Palmerston North, and the road I was following, to the north and east. Even though I had only ridden a short distance it was an interesting place to stop.

> THIS MEMORIAL
> ON THE SITE OF THE FORMER POLISH CHILDREN'S CAMP,
> WAS ERECTED BY THE POLISH COMMUNITY
> IN APPRECIATION OF THE SHELTER GIVEN
> BY THE PEOPLE OF NEW ZEALAND
> TO 734 POLISH CHILDREN IN 1944.
> IN WORLD WAR 2 THEY SURVIVED
> DEPORTATION TO SIBERIA
> AND AFTER A TEMPORARY STAY IN IRAN,
> FOUND IN THIS COUNTRY
> HOME, FRIENDS AND SECURITY.
> 22 FEBRUARY, 1975

The town campsite had a sign asking campers to go to the filling station down the road. Once there, for a deposit of 20 dollars I was given a key for the showers and toilets, and had to pay a further 5 for the camping. Unlike most NZ campsites, there was no kitchen so I had to dig out my stove. But, this was very good value for a place near the town centre. I walked around the corner and bought a secondhand book, sat in the shade all afternoon, reading. On the wall, there was an interesting Groucho Marx quote: "Outside of a dog, a book is a man's best friend."

Later, I was joined by two blokes who were in Woodville for a tennis tournament and another guy who offered me a cup of tea. While drinking the tea, I listened to him telling me all about his heart problems – he was waiting for a transplant, and was worried that he might loose his license. By the description he gave me, I was surprised he still had a license to loose.

Steady climb

The road climbed away north and the next large town gave no one any doubt about its origins. Dannevirke, had a big Viking signpost at its entrance.

The Danish workers came over early in the 19th century after a confrontation with the Saxons and built this town. I had a very good apple crumble with my coffee for my morning break. A short distance further on was the village of Norsewood that too sounded as if there was some sort of Danish link.

Along this long stretch of road, helped by the wind, but sometimes annoyed by rumble strips, which from time to time in NZ, can be a bloody nuisance and even dangerous at times when very badly positioned.

Also along this stretch there was little problem finding campsites, as every little town seemed to have one.

Once close to Hastings the roads suddenly had traffic. Last time I wandered around the place looking at the earth movement that resulted from the 1931 earthquake, this time I didn't, and headed towards Napier. As I remember it, the road then just continued around the coast on the 2. This time there was a choice of road, and I attempted to follow the same route as last time, and followed the signs to Clive.
I only remember that because my brother's name is Clive. It wasn't named after him, as I know he has never been there. It was most likely named after Clive of India – but he didn't go there either!

Clive

Clive bridge

Clive has a little shop, a fish and chips place, a campsite and a river. I crossed over the bridge and followed a coastal cycle path, in the rain, to Napier.

Wet wooden cycle path in Napier.

Overcast Napier

Out of Napier, for a short distance, the 2 clings to the coast before heading NW to Lake Taupo; or closer to the coast, my route, towards Gisberne. Either way there are lots of climbs, but even so I got a surprise. Just after where the road hugs the coast I saw a campsite sign, and decided to have a look.

The little road wound up a mountainside, and climbed and climbed before eventually dropping down to the coast a long way from the main road, at Waipatiki Beach.

Looking down towards the sea.

An expensive, but interesting, farm campsite, was where I, with jelly like legs, camped for the night had people leaving at the end of the holidays.

Instead of following the tarmac road over the mountain and back the 12km to the main road (the way I had come), then climb over the pass on the 2, it was suggested I should take a gravel road from the top of the mountain, and follow it to the pass. Although I didn't much like the sound of this idea, I tried it, and it worked really well. Not that this was the end of the climbing, this is another very hilly area. At the top of one great climb is a lake. I stopped to take some pictures, and was joined by one of the many clubs for old cars, this time it was Austins. There were all sorts and ages of production cars and some specials. I was about to take a picture, but found the battery in my iPhone was flat. I suppose it was silly to go on a trip like this without my camera. The original plan had been to charge everything from the bike, and that option wasn't now available. I decided I would buy a camera at the next big town.

This bit of the 2 is called the Pacific Coast Highway, but it wanders around the hills with little sign of the coast until Waihua.

At the campsite at Wairoa, I again met the Austin car club, it seems they were driving little more each day than I was riding.

For some time I had been having some trouble with my old Garmin. It would change the pr-set functions at will, and now it was refusing to recognize the charging method I was using – any of them, the i-phone devise, the battery storage, or its even own bog standard charger. Sometimes it would start to charge, then stop charging, but stay switched on, and drain its own battery. In short, the simple distance recorder I had in the 80's would have been better.

At Morere, just before a long tough climb, is a little café and campsite. It was here I met a man whose job was to cull the feral goat population. It was a most interesting chat. He would be dropped off into the wild by helicopter, where he would keep shooting these wild goats until he ran out of ammunition. It was interesting for two reasons: a very big male had almost hit me as it bounded into the traffic that morning; and in the 1950s my Uncle Alvis, for part of the year, would cull deer, but without the helicopter. Alvis, who died recently, had led a wild life, and while he was in NZ attempted the world record for the highest parachute jump without oxygen. It failed, the plane couldn't't get up high enough. However, he did break the Australasian record for the longest free-fall and highest jump. Culling deer did seem to fit in with his way of life at that time.

It was after a lot of climbing that the road descended into Gisborne. I spent some time looking for a photography shop, found one, but they no longer sold cameras! It seems they can't compete with the big stores. So, in the end, I went to a big store and bought a small camera so that I didn't have the constant problem of both trying to get my iPhone and Garmin charged each day. I then went on a foolish spree of taking trial pictures, before realizing there was no memory card in my wonderful new camera!

NE from Gisborne

The Eastern Cape is a bit out of the way for many New Zealanders. Jess, the elder brother of Alvis, was a keen climber, and he had even been on the 1956 Ed Hilary crossing of Antarctica – if only to the base camp; but on my last trip he told me he had never been to the Eastern Cape. This made it seem a very desirable place to go for some reason. It proved to be remote, wild, and very attractive. A definite attraction for my latest tour too.

The ride around the Cape is a constant mix of flat coastal bays, and tough hills.

The population around these often stunning coastal stretches is usually quite small. There is holiday traffic and logging trucks, but not too much work for locals. It is not the best place to stock up with food supplies, as the further around the Cape, the more remote it seems, and the last chance there is to find a shop.

Tokomararu Bay campsite was a bit rundown but fine for one-night campers like me. It did have its own little fish shop where I paid a very modest camp fee. I was to learn later that someone else had bought the fish shop, so there would be future changes.

The next day started with a very tough climb before dropping down to Puia Springs, where, at a filling station, I bought a pie and coffee. Near the top of the climb a large eagle took to the air quite close to me.

A guy in the filling station described the road ahead as dead flat. When it was't going up or down, it was! To be fair to him, the last bit into Te Araroa was a bit easier than much of this road.

At the campsite in Te Araroa I met a cyclist travelling around the Cape in the opposite direction to me. This was useful as we were able to pass on road conditions and campsite information to each other. Gay was like me a retired teacher, but unlike me, a Kiwi and a woman. Oddly on this trip, as opposed to the last one, when most of the cyclists were local men, most of the cycle tourists I met this time were from overseas and a mixture of men an women.

I had camped, on a nice bit of grass, quite close to a huge tree. Just as I had got nicely settled in, I was told the log my bike was parked against had fallen from the tree, and I should move my tent. Although I didn't think another huge log would fall my way, I moved.

Gay, my bike and the fallen log.

Climbing away away from one bay I would often get a view of the next one way below.

In one remote spot on top of a hill, miles from anywhere, a chicken popped out of cover to look at me.

The school holidays were now over, so the tourist trade had dropped off.

The last few tourists

On scattered beaches there were still some tourists

As the road stuck closer to the coast and headed more to the south, the hills became much less severe, but at the same time it was getting hotter and hotter. The sun in NZ can be wonderful, but because of all the time I spend cycling in hot climates, I am very keen to keep putting on the sun block. Along this coast I plastered on plenty.

The odd fisherman and bold trees.

The road would still go backwards and forwards around rivers and their bridges, but this was all very pleasant cycling.

River estuary and bridge crossing.

One thing that stands out above everything else around this area, is the Maori tradition captured in their wood carvings.

There is a thousand years of Maori history before 1769, when Captain Cook visited the islands. Opotiki was a populous Maori centre, but it's not correct to think of the Maoris as one great culture before the Europeans arrived, as there were many rival groups, who were likely to have arrived in NZ at different times.

Opotiki town centre

Warning against running over a rare bird only to find they turn up at the campsite!

It is a very rare thing, when you see a sign warning you not to run over that rare thing, then you see one dead on the road, then shortly afterwards at the campsite, you see what looked like a group of them dashing for the bushes, with two hanging back for a distant photo shot!

Unlike Australia, South Africa or North America, there was no policy to wipe out earlier residents, but this does not imply there were no problems at all. In this part of NZ, in 1840s and 50s, land ownership and religion sparked off murder and retribution on a grand scale.

Leaving the 2 just before Whakatane, and following a coast of salt marshes, where mussels were being sold, was a better option than sticking to the main road. The intention was to continue closer to the coast on the 30, but finding, after crossing the harbour on a cycle path alongside the bridge, I was heading south instead of west I decided not to bother going back to Whakatane, but to rejoin and follow the 2 again.

Mussel stall.

Marshland

When I reached the coast again there was a campsite at Matata, as this was a bit too soon to stop, despite the feeling there was one hell of a storm brewing, I plodded on thinking that on a road next to the sea I would soon see another campsite.

It was quite a long ride and a move away from the coast before I saw a campsite sign directing me to Maketu Bay.

Being on the 2 again was short lived as I neared Tauranga, once again I found I was heading for a motorway. A marked cycle route took me to a small coast road, before the signs dried up completely.

Coming out onto the correct road beyond the town was very hit and miss.

The cycle-path clings to the side of the bridge.
That evening, having had waterproofs on all day, I was back on the coast at Athenree.
I did manage to get the tent up before the real storm hit. Putting extra pegs in all around the tent, and big rocks on the guy ropes at either end, yet I still wasn't fully prepared for what did hit the campsite. It was the tail end of the typhoon that had wiped out towns on several Fiji islands. The tent swayed around all night, as the gale blasted and howled in from the sea, but it kept me dry and warm inside. What more could I ask?

Storm!

I was now at the point on my first trip that I realised there was no time to explore the area north of Auckland, and I made my way in the direction of the airport. This time I could manage some time further north, but not make it all the way to the tip of North Island.

Looking at the map, I felt I should be able to get a boat from Coromande to somewhere north of Auckland, and, if this was the case, either follow the 25 up the east side of the Coromandel Peninsula, or the 26 up the west. I chose the latter. This choice took me along what, without the constant road repairs and traffic lights, would have been a very attractive gulley to the 26 turnoff to Thames.

Near Thames

Along a rugged coast, just to the north of Thames, I found a sign to a campsite. I ended on a wet nasty pitch away from all the facilities, and in the rain had no desire to wander around much.

In the morning, for the second time on this trip, I wished I had bought some lights to replace my aircraft damaged set. It was not only overcast, but I was on a narrow, winding road, with no hard shoulder, and a drop on the left down to the sea. Some rocks had been washed down from the cliffs on the right and blocked the drains that ran under the road, leaving a series of local, rideable, floods.

Despite this, it was a wonderfully attractive coastline. The up and down, twisting climbs, were easy to ride, and once in a while there was a safe stopping place to admire the view. Just before Coromande the road did provide a double shock to the system, one long climb, and after dropping down, followed by an equally long climb.

The Information Office in Coromanda provided a bigger shock than the climbs. South of the town, on a spur from the road I came in on, there was a ferry to Auckland that evening at 9pm.

The only way to get to the road north was to then take a local ferry north to Devenport. As I had a book, and there were pleasant places to sit out of the now strong sunshine for five hours or so, that didn't turn out to be the problem.

That came when, sitting in the dark on a jetty with just a few people fishing, I found the ferry had broken down at Ponui Island. It did eventually pick me up, take me and a few others back to Ponui Island, and then on to Aukland.

As I was told there were lots of good value places to stay near the docks, I wasn't too concerned. There were, plenty of Backpacker places, but they were all full. There were also a lot of modest priced places, they too were full. Walking around from one big hotel to the next, I found they too were fully booked. It seems there were all sorts of things all happening at once, and the whole city was booked up.

TV – my room

By the time I found a room in the very expensive Sky Tower, it was almost time to get up again.

Devenport ferry

The ferry to Devenport didn't take long, and after a wander around I found the road north, this was the 1, and once again it was a motorway. However, there was a coastal route north that ran almost parallel, and was very much more mountainous, east of the motorway. Although a tough ride this had a clear advantage over the main road, it was attractive.

Distant motorway

 At one moment the road ran alongside a holiday beach, and then I would be looking down at the motorway in the valley way below.

Suddenly, my enjoyable route came to an end, it swept down a long climb and joined the 1, which was no longer a motorway, but still looked like one.

After about 25km of main road riding I saw a sign for the town of Warkworth. As the place looked big enough for a campsite, and I was feeling very tired, the place was well worth a visit. The information office was very helpful.

There was no campsite in town, but if I continued along the main route for four or five kilometres, there was a place called Sheep World, and I could camp there. This turned out to be a very different sort of campsite. It was a working farm with a café, but the café belonged to someone else, and they closed early. Had I been there in the daytime when there were children, I'm sure I could have watched sheep loosing their winter woolies, but I wasn't.

The pond

There were several other people camping including a couple of guys I got on well with. One was from Finland and the other from Sweden. Next to my tent was a toilet, shower and TV room. To get to a double-small kitchen, and sheltered outdoor places to eat food, there was a short walk along a pathway between hedges. Just beyond all this was a pond, then a forested hillside. Everything I could want was there – just a bit different.

Eating area

Riding along on the route 1 is not my idea of a perfect cycle ride. It was bloody hot, the hard shoulder wasn't always wide enough, and every now and then, my pet hate, rumble strips. Once in a while, there was a turnoff to a village that I took advantage of. The day ended at a campsite on the edge of Whangarei. That afternoon, it was a long walk in the hot sunshine to a supermarket in the town centre. I was very pleased to stock up with supplies as I was running short of almost everything.

Despite some fantastic coastal spots, I wasn't enjoying my ride north of Auckland as much as the rest of the ride. It seemed to me that the traffic had the big city mentality of only being a few hundred kilometres from Auckland, and being able to speed back there at the end of the day. After a day on what was now the *Twin Coast Discovery Highway,* I was keen to find out what the other twin looked like. I took a loop down to Paihia on the coast, with the aim of crossing over to the west coast the next day. It turned out to be a very attractive, but tough loop to ride around. I was very pleased to find a campsite with a splendid view over a bay.

Sunset from the campsite

Along this coast it didn't take long before my legs were tested before being rewarded by more fantastic coastline. However, I was soon climbing away from the coast and back to the ugly sister of the *Twin Coastal Highway,* hoping for a beautiful princess for my ride to the west coast and then the south. Even if the main route north had been more desirable, time had run out and the dash to the airport couldn't be delayed.

Last look at the east coast before heading west

Away from the route north it soon became much quieter, and far more pleasant. After a breakfast stop in the quiet large town of Kaikobe, I was soon out in the open countryside again, where cows would cross the road as they were moved from field to field.

The road to Opononi was extremely enjoyable, possibly more so by being free of almost motorway conditions over the previous couple of days. One small sting in the tail was a climb just before Opononi when I wanted a drink and a snack and shade from the hot sunshine. I couldn't find shade, but I did sit by the road and enjoy an energy bar and some water.

One by one, small groups of cyclists, all equipped with very basic camping equipment, rode by. I caught one group that had stopped on the top of the hill; I was to see more of them later at the campsite in Opononi. It seems they were riding on an end to end of NZ trial. All of them were fitted with a chip so the organizers could trace then along the route.

On the campsite I had a spot overlooking the water from some height. Opononi really is a pleasant place to camp. The route south, although still *The Twin Coast Highway* was as different from the main road north as it was possible to be. I now had to get further south, and fairly quickly if I was to catch my flight.

Opononi

This was going to be a day of even more climbing than usual. Some of the end-to-end riders who had been at the same campsite as me were up and away early, some before first light. As I tackled the first long climb a rider came dashing past. "Sorry, I can't Stop," he yelled, "I have to catch the boat".

I later found these cyclists had a route to follow, and special boats were put on twice a day to take them over stretches of water where there was no regular crossing point. This guy was trying to get the next boat from Pouto, and avoid having to wait another 12hrs.

I was in no such rush, and after the climb had a coffee break at Wamamaku. In both Australia and NZ it is common to have signs to tell people to wear shoes in the restaurant, but this sign was different.

In earlier times this roadside café had been a cheese factory, but the world had moved on.

The road kept winding up to a forest. It was a tough but pleasant ride, and to my surprise, a group of the cyclists who had left at the crack of dawn were having a snack next to a forest path to a famous tree. I wandered down to have a look. The *Lord of the forest* is 51.5m tall and has a trunk girth of 13.8m, and it is estimated to be 2,000 years old. No, I didn't go to its birthday party and measure it - I just read the sign.

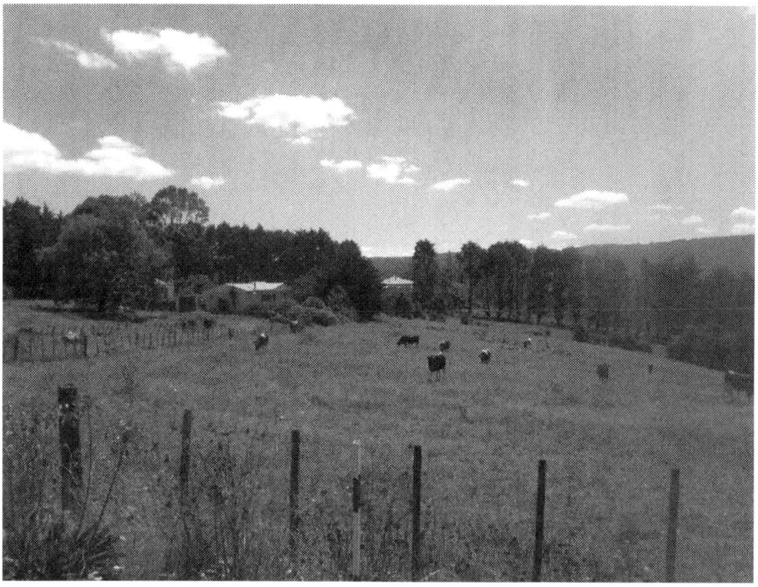

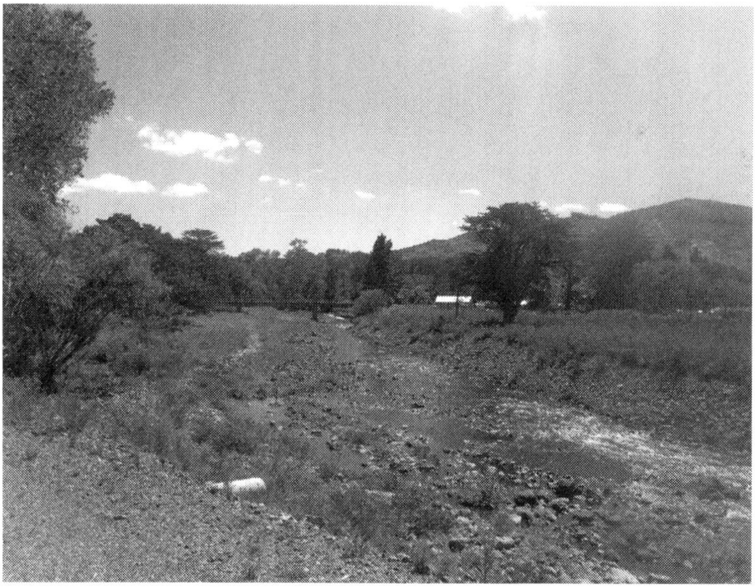

Beyond this point, although the road was still very much up and down, it was now much easier. All the way to Dargaville, where I camped for the night, I kept catching end-to-end cyclists. Having just ridden 5,000km was giving me some sort of edge. In the little shop in Dargaville, one of the older members of the end-to-end group had slept all day there. Some of the others were to camp at the same place as me; others were pushing on to catch the next boat. It was suggested to me that I should try and get on their boat and take a much more direct route to Auckland. This wasn't a sound option for me, because had they not let me use the boat, getting to the airport on time would be even more difficult.

I was looking forward to riding alongside a great stretch of the Wairoa River on the 42, unfortunately, I hadn't bargained for a thick mist clinging to the water. Later a wind picked up and pushed me along making the climbs a pleasure, but leaving the river a long way behind and below. By the time I reached the 1 again, it was hot and not nearly so pleasant. Fortunately the wind still gently pushed me along, and it wasn't a bad ride, despite the traffic. At Wellstone, having done well over 100km, it was time to look for a campsite. The 16, that headed down the west coast, looked the most attractive option, but I was told there was no places to stay for a considerable distance along that route, so the best option was to head for Sheep World, where I knew there was a campsite. Feeling very dehydrated after a day in the hot sun, with all three bottles near empty, I bought 2 one-litre bottles of milk, drank one on the spot, and packed the other for Sheep world. Spending my second night there, I was treated like a long lost friend.

From Sheep World it is not that far to Auckland if your in a car heading down the motorway, and for the first 20km or so it was the same for me, before it became a proper motorway, and I had to climb up to the hills above the coastline.

Above the east coast

In the main I followed the same route as on the way north, and ended up at the Devenport ferry.

Although I had heard that the 20 also became a motorway but had a cycle route alongside, this wasn't the time to experiment. Auckland is built around water and to move anywhere, ways across the water have to be found.

Once in the city centre I headed south until, after some wandering around, I did get myself onto a difficult to follow cycle route heading in the direction of the airport, but missed the South Road I was looking for, and had to wander around little more until I found it and the campsite. By that time, a day of showers had turned into a heavy downpour.

From the cycle path following the 20.

I set off early the next morning to get to the airport both before the forecasted storm, and so I had plenty of time to sort out a bike box. The latter turned out to be easy, and my bike was soon packed and labeled for Manchester, thanks to me packing the notched wood I had used when I changed the tyres around.

On my last trip, 30 years ago, it was just a case of letting the air out of the tyres, and it was returned to me in Sydney, where I stayed overnight at a campsite – and had an interesting adventure, before my onward flight to PNG.

Perhaps now is the time to answer the question I asked myself at the start of this journey:

Would I still recognise the places I also fondly remembered from last time?

Well, not many, perhaps because my route had small (and some large) changes all the way.

Was the Backwind all the way *theory of 30 years ago just a fond memory and perhaps an illusion?*

This didn't stand up as a 100% rule, but while I was on the old route it did stand up quite well. But the fact was, because the road conditions had changed so much, I wasn't able to follow the old route.

On the first ride it took only the six-week school holiday. Being older, and retired, this time I was able to take much longer, and ride a little bit further, and slower, and took two and a half months.

For those that require some idea of distance, Christchurch was about 1,500km from Auckland, Invercargill almost 2,000km, Nelson over 3,000km, the Bay of Islands over 4,000 and the total ride, 5,000km.

Camping with a tent again proved to be the best option. There were many places where all hotels and motels were fully booked, but I always managed to find a camping spot, even in areas full of tourists, with the exception of Auckland.

On thing is certain, NZ is a fantastic country to cycle around now, just as it was then.

If I was to cycle around again next year, what would I change?

My gear ratios were about right, with a bottom of 27", was perfect for most of the ride. Just once in a while, at the top of a long steep hill, a slightly lower ratio might help.

I wouldn't take my Garmin – finding my way in NZ is no problem, and it would be one less thing to charge up.

I didn't take a back up camera to my iPhone, and ended up buying one.

Being someone that uses a phone only to take pictures, I didn't use an app or even a website – perhaps I should have. If they had been available 30 years ago when I was in my mid 40s, I might have. I suspect it's an age thing...

There is also a cycle trail guide: www.nzcycletrail.com

Paul Davenport

From the aged 11, when I received my first bicycle, no relative within 100 miles could avoid me turning up their doorstep. In order to keep family harmony, it became necessary for me to join a cycle club. From then on cycling began to take over my life. I would read anything about cycling, and spent my spare time either riding or repairing bicycles.

As I got older I took part in all forms of competitive cycling across Europe, but my main love was to wander off with little more than a tent and a change of clothing. I had a deep desire to see the world.

Ten years spent in the military did help me reach distant parts not previously available. Having a better than average fitness enabled me to become one of the few people from the Intelligence Corps to pass SAS selection and, once armed with this greater knowledge of coping with extreme environments, I became even more adventurous. Later as a teacher, during the holidays, I took young people to the wilder parts of Britain as a CTC assessor for their Duke of Edinburgh Gold Award.

For 25 years, mainly teaching in international schools, I wandered the globe. Although best known for more extreme journeys, I have a deep affection for the gentle routes that cover much of Europe.

Also by Paul Davenport:
Bike it to Budapest,
The Cycle Camper
Australasia – Part 1 – New Zealand
Part 2 – Australia
Africa – A Cyclist's Safari

Printed in Poland
by Amazon Fulfillment
Poland Sp. z o.o., Wrocław